FORGET-ME-NOT-CHILD

Angela McClusky comes with her adopted family to Birmingham after fleeing the terrible poverty in Ireland, but their dreams of a better life are ruined as misfortune follows them. When Angela marries her childhood sweetheart, she has hopes of a brighter future, but her husband is called up to fight in the Great War. Tragedy strikes and Angela is left to rear her frail daughter on her own, though the worst is yet to come when Angela suffers another terrible misfortune. As the terrible conflict drags on for years with little contact from the men sent off to fight, can Angela find the courage to face so many hardships alone?